Amazing Champion of the Earth

RACHEL CARSON

Mary Dodson Wade

AMAZING AMERICANS

Enslow Elementary

an imprint of

Enslow Publishers, Inc.

40 Industrial Road
Box 398
Berkeley Heights, NJ 07922
USA

http://www.enslow.com

Enslow Elementary, an imprint of Enslow Publishers, Inc.
Enslow Elementary® is a registered trademark of Enslow Publishers, Inc.

Library of Congress Cataloging-in-Publication Data

Wade, Mary Dodson.
    Amazing champion of the earth Rachel Carson / Mary Dodson Wade.
       p. cm. — (Amazing Americans)
    Includes index.
    Summary: "This entry-level biography introduces readers to Rachel Carson, who wrote about why we
need to protect the environment"—Provided by publisher.
    ISBN-13: 978-0-7660-3283-5
    ISBN-10: 0-7660-3283-3
    1. Carson, Rachel, 1907–1964—Juvenile literature. 2. Biologists—United States—Biography—Juvenile
literature. 3. Environmentalists—United States—Biography—Juvenile literature. I. Title.
    QH31.C33W33 2009
    333.95'16092--dc22
    [B]
                     2008024891

Printed in the United States of America

10 9 8 7 6 5 4 3 2 1

Illustration Credits: Associated Press, p. 16 (right); Bill Cannon, p. 19; By Permission of Rachel Carson Council, Inc., pp. 4, 8; The Granger Collection, p. 16 (left); National Oceanic and Atmospheric Administration, p. 12; Rachel Carson Collection, College Archives, Chatham University, p. 7; U.S. Fish and Wildlife Service, pp. 11, 15.

Cover Illustration: Bill Cannon (Wildlife Refuge); National Oceanic and Atmospheric Administration (Rachel Carson)

Caption: Rachel Carson's official Fish and Wildlife Service photo.

0710

CONTENTS

Growing Up

Rachel Carson was born in 1907 on a Pennsylvania farm. The quiet little girl loved to explore the woods. She grew up to be a famous writer. Her strong words would change the way people treat our environment. No one had ever written about this before.

◀ Rachel, sitting on her mother's lap, with her sister, Marian, and her brother, Robert.

When Rachel was young, her mother read nature stories to her. Rachel wrote her own stories. A magazine paid her $10 for a story. She was only 10 years old.

Rachel went to college to study writing. Then Rachel took a science class. She changed her mind. Now she would be a scientist *and* a writer!

Rachel Carson graduated from ►
college in 1929.

In 1936, Rachel got a job with the government in Washington, D.C. She wrote booklets about fish.

Then Rachel wrote a report about ocean animals. It was so good that a popular magazine bought it. Rachel wrote more. Soon she had written *Under the Sea-Wind*, her first book.

Rachel Carson wrote booklets like this one ▶ when she worked for the government.

CONSERVATION IN ACTION

GUARDING OUR WILDLIFE RESOURCES

Number FIVE
Fish and Wildlife Service, United States Department of the Interior, Washington, D. C.

CHAPTER 3

Writing *The Sea Around Us*

Rachel wanted to write more books about the ocean. A famous scientist told her to go deep-sea diving. She laughed. She was not a good swimmer! But she went diving to learn more about the ocean.

Rachel worked during the day. She wrote at night. She lived with her mother, who was more than 80 years old. Her mother typed the pages for Rachel's second book.

◄ Rachel Carson was one of the first women to sail on this boat, the *Albatross III*.

The Sea Around Us was a best seller. It was made into a movie. The movie won an award.

By 1952, Rachel had enough money to quit work. She bought a house in Maine. She walked the beaches and woods. She kept writing.

Rachel Carson, and her co-worker, Bob Hines, look ▶ at something in the water in Florida in 1952.

CHAPTER 4

Silent Spring

One day Rachel got a letter from a friend. All the song birds around her house had died. Rachel learned why the birds died. They had eaten insects that were poisoned by pesticides.

Rachel wrote about this in her book, *Silent Spring*.

◄ *Silent Spring* is one of Rachel's most famous books (above). These men are spraying DDT, a type of pesticide, to kill the spruce bud worm that is hurting the trees (below).

Pesticide companies did not like her book. They did not want people to stop buying pesticides. They said Rachel was wrong. President Kennedy asked scientists to find out the truth. Rachel was right!

Rachel Carson died in 1964. She was 56 years old. Today, her words still remind us of the beauty of nature and how we need to protect it.

The Rachel Carson National Wildlife Refuge in Maine was created to protect salt marshes for birds and other animals. ▶

Something to Think About

Rachel Carson said that if we looked at the beauty of nature, we would not want to destroy it.

Her sister's grandson came to live with her. They took walks together. They found tiny sea animals at the edge of the ocean. The little boy could look at them. Then he had to put them back where he found them.

Why did she have him do that?

In 1980 Rachel Carson was given the Presidential Medal of Honor for her work in saving nature.

What can you do to make your home or school a better place?

TIMELINE

1907—May 27, born on a farm near Springdale, Pennsylvania.

1917—Sold a story to *St. Nicholas* magazine for $10.

1932—Worked at the U. S. Bureau of Fisheries writing about fish.

1937—*Atlantic Monthly* magazine bought "Undersea."

1941—Wrote first book, *Under the Sea-Wind.*

1951—Wrote second book, a best-seller called *The Sea Around Us.*

1955—Wrote third book, *The Edge of the Sea.*

1962—Wrote fourth book, *Silent Spring.*

1964—April 14, died.

WORDS TO KNOW

deep-sea diving—Going to the deeper parts of the ocean.

environment—Our surroundings: the air, water, plants, animals, and the Earth.

pesticides—Chemicals used to kill bugs and other pests.

scientist—A person who studies science to learn new things.

☆LEARN MORE

BOOKS

Ehrlich, Amy. *Rachel: The Story of Rachel Carson*.
San Diego: Harcourt/Silver Whistle, 2003.

Fontes, Justine and Ron Fontes. *Rachel Carson*.
Chicago: Children's Press, 2005.

INTERNET ADDRESSES

The Rachel Carson Homestead, Springdale, PA
http://www.rachelcarsonhomestead.org

The Rachel Carson National Wildlife Refuge
http://rachelcarson.fws.gov

PLACES TO VISIT

Rachel Carson Homestead
613 Marion Ave
Springdale, PA 15144

 INDEX